# of sun and snow

K. Strawbridge

BookLeaf Publishing

Presentation by *BookLeaf Publishing*

Web: www.bookleafpub.com

E-mail: info@bookleafpub.com

ISBN: 9789357444712

First edition 2023

For my parents.

I love you.

ACKNOWLEDGEMENT

To my family, my friends, my village - you mean the world to me. I wouldn't be here without you lifting me up when I couldn't stand, and loving me enough to keep me on my feet.

Thank you.

Summer

i remember being in your arms
when the air last clung to me
like this
like you

the birds in the trees
sing to the sun
their melodies so sweet
i can't hear them

i feel your hands
and your voice
and how wrong this must be
it's wrong, right?

blue skies blind
the heat beats down
the air clings to me
i wish i wish it was you

somewhere new

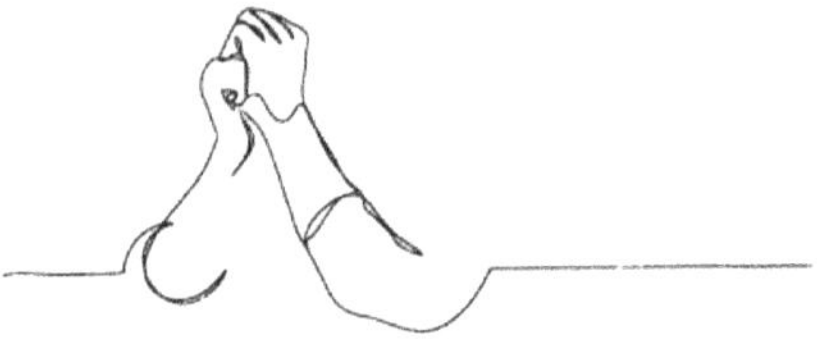

take me somewhere new
where the light solely gives
cobbled streets shining seas
show me where the happy lives

i want to watch the sunset
and hear children laugh
drive too fast and sing too loud
as the world goes dark

i want to see it all
paint and write and run
feel the air in my lungs
let it all go, just for one

there's all this new
waiting out there for me
why would i want to stay here?
tell me

why do i want to stay here?

relay

it wasn't your fault
you didn't mean it

i find those words running a relay race
round and round and round my mind

it wasn't your fault
you didn't mean it

so i keep forgiving you
despite my tears
and my hands shaking
and the kind woman asking
"how has your week been?"

it wasn't your fault
you really didn't mean it

i keep forgiving you
using words i heard
between your silence
as if you need it
as if you deserve it

do you?
do you deserve it?

and even if you do
did i?

artefact

we're smiling in this polaroid
frozen in peace
suspended in space
an artefact of another time

i think we deserve
to be treated as such

we were beautiful
made for museums
to be seen
not touched

beheld
from behind the glass

all i need

after the calm
after the storm
once i resurface, and turn to the sky

when my body shakes
salt stains my skin
and my thoughts twist tirelessly
around my heart

i will hold my own hand
whisper my own sweet words
wash my own wounds

i am my lighthouse
i am my waves
i am all i will ever need

Autumn

there's something about autumn
unplanned, unrehearsed, undone
the trees fall apart and we trust completely that
we will see them in full bloom once again

there is an unrelenting permission
to let go
to allow yourself to crumble, break
and while you fall to the floor
the birds will see only beauty
in your tumbling colours

because you'll be back
just like the trees
beginning again, like clockwork
gold to green

take aim

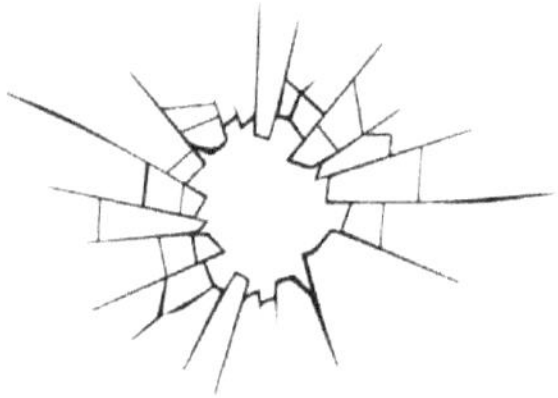

it was chaos
shouting screaming pleading
the gunshot rang out
the poor souls dropped

caught in the crossfire, but were we
if we started the war?
though i never felt
that we wanted it at all

please
stay down
we can't go on like this
stay down

the memory is hazy
we both took aim
and i know
i shot back

but did i shoot first?

giant

it's scary,
this growing up stuff

i can feel myself outgrowing my bedroom
pressing against the walls
my head brushing the ceiling

but it's peaceful here
and safe

and who knows what's out there
bundled in the blankets
of my next bedroom

it's scary
i'd like to stay here
can i stay here?

safety blanket

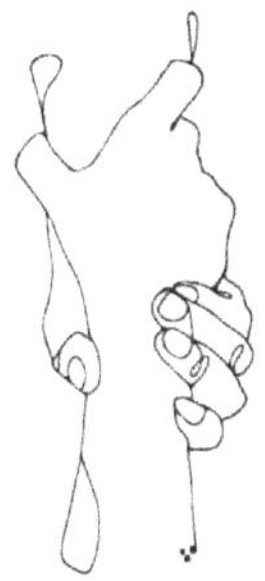

my best friend moved away
she called me today
said she has no safety blanket
no one to catch her fall

so i went and picked her up a blanket
woven, soft, chosen to match her room

she says people
are her safe haven
and i am part of her home
but for now, i cannot be with her

so, instead,
i'll imbue all of me into this wool

and i'll pray that she feels it
the love and pride and warmth
all the things i cannot tell her
all the things she deserves

and i'll pray when she wraps it around her
she hears me say

i'll always catch her fall

rear view

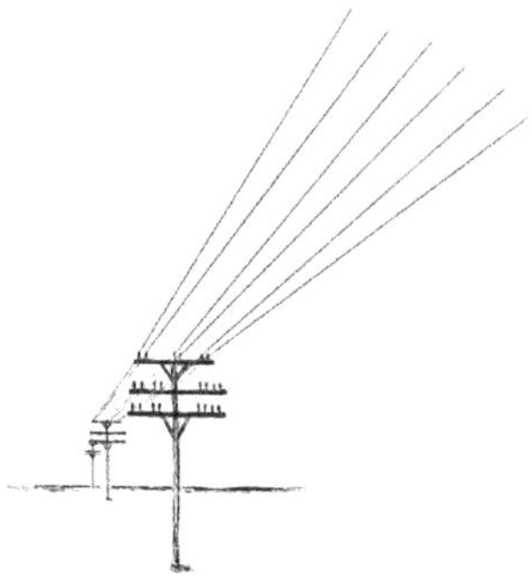

i wonder if i'll ever figure out
when i'm using too much of my heart
or too much of my head

will i ever know before
what my battered heart deserves
and see through the stars in the night

can i ever learn in time
when my mind should stand firm
to lead me from blushing fogs

the sky in my rear view mirror is always
unclouded
but my windscreen never clears

Winter

it's that time of year again
when my breath makes little clouds
swirling and spiralling
into the sky

i've always said i can breathe easier
in the cold
my lungs feel lighter
not weighed down in warmth

this year i've felt it the most
but this time
as i watch the air materialise
i have to wonder

is it really the frost
that makes my heart beat easier
or, maybe, just maybe
is it the lack of you?

dandelion

my therapist likened thoughts to clouds
a few days ago

fluffy, white, grey, black
solid and real
floating overhead
but if we were to touch them

our hands would go straight through
for, really, they aren't anything at all

just a collection of water vapour

if we treat thoughts the same, she said
they will also pass us by

how strange
i thought
that something so not real
can create our entire world

our minds balance on dandelion seeds
float in universes of our own creation

how strange indeed

ghost

i'm not sure when i became
a ghost

this out of order sign
on my doorway
this body adorned in
rotting fairy houses

i didn't want them
to see this

so i've sat in this
haunted house
bound to myself
for months

transparent
(only literally)

i'd like to say hello again
but i'm not sure
if anyone
could hear

you

it's funny that
even after everything
after all that mess
i still think about that morning

it was early
the glow through the glass was soft
like snow
i'd gotten up, turned back to you

and there you sat
dark hair tousled
bird songs in your eyes
your freckles dancing across your cheeks

you always covered them up
hid them away
locked up tight with the rest of you
i never did get why

but in those mornings
where you smiled
and your freckles crinkled with your eyes
i remember i thought

the poets meant you, every time

clean

the sun through the window
glints and glares
creates sonnets in my
darkest footpaths

each press of my sole
into the soft ground
leaves it's mark
i carry it until it washes away

you know
i only read the words left
behind
i cannot explain it to you

the sun dries the soil
into my shoes
only the river
can make me clean

Spring

good morning, my love

the sun is rising over the rooftops
planting seeds of warmth in the air
glazing the concrete with honeydew drops
the world born new, all is fair

it's peaceful

a chance to bloom
with this earth
a chance to start
all over again

midas

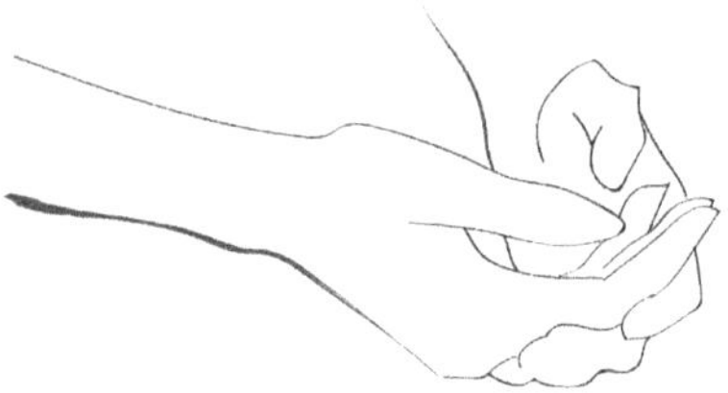

rings of silver
wrapped tight around my fingers
shining, shimmering
a weight to comfort in the dark

but in the light i saw it
the boa wrapping
around around around
sleep now

and in the wake
my hands were bare
and from the glow
an altar was born

in midas' name

rings of gold
wrapped right around my fingers
shining, shimmering
no weight at all

choices

you deserve to choose yourself

even when they want you
even when they need you
even when the harshest hands
tear you at the seams

you cannot help anyone else
when your own walls press too close
you cannot heal anyone else
without first dealing your own dose

give it a try
bandage your own wounds
breathe air back into your own lungs
no one else will do it for you

remember
you are the only person
with everlasting permission
to choose you

and more choices

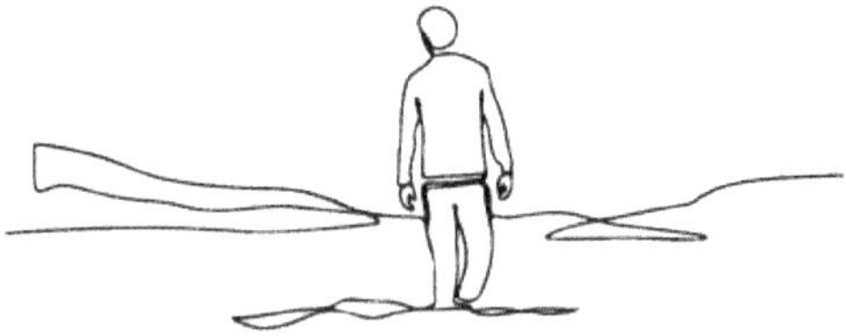

choices
i was always meant to have them
operative word
“meant”

what do you want?
me?
well
what do i need?

no
what would you like to do
to be
where would you like to go?

i don’t know

i get to choose now
and i get to be safe
in whatever i want
just like all of you

that’s new

bluebird day

i caught your perfume in the
air the other day
i whipped my head around
to catch your ghost
in the crowd

you weren’t there
the mind loves to play
tricks
i guess
and i wasn’t sure i wanted you to be

no, scratch that
i didn’t want you to be
for the first time
i turned into your scent
and the birds

didn’t sing

revolution

i ran the same lap
for too long
i think

at some point
i had to move to the next
to let it go

and in doing so
i saw those who had run
every revolution

with me
in the searing rain
and i finally felt that love

the hurt
cannot follow me
forever

but
god
the love can

www.ingramcontent.com/pod-product-compliance
Lightning Source LLC
Chambersburg PA
CBHW051753130826
49812CB00033B/1134
* 9 7 8 9 3 5 7 4 4 4 7 1 2 *